Esquire

THINGS A

MAN

SHOULD KNOW ABOUT

MARRIAGE

Also available in this series:

Things a Man Should Know About Style

Esquire's THINGS A **MAN** SHOULD KNOW ABOUT MARRIAGE

Scott Omelianuk
and Ted Allen

RIVERHEAD BOOKS, NEW YORK

Riverhead Books
Published by The Berkley Publishing Group
A division of Penguin Putnam Inc.
375 Hudson Street
New York, New York 10014

Book design by Pauline Neuwirth, Neuwirth & Associates, Inc.
Photographs by Brian Velenchenko
Photo editing by Ian Spanier
Styling by Severin and Louise Godwin for Tiffany Whitford, NYC

First edition: December 1999

The Penguin Putnam Inc. World Wide Web site address is
http://www.penguinputnam.com

Library of Congress Cataloging-in-Publication Data
Omelianuk, Scott.
      Esquire's things a man should know about marriage / Scott Omelianuk
    and Ted Allen. — 1st ed.
        p.   cm.
      ISBN 1-57322-777-3
      1. Marriage—Humor. 2. Weddings—Humor. 3. Man–woman relationships—Humor.
    I. Title: Things a man should know about marriage. II. Allen, Ted. III. Title.
    PN6231.M3O44   1999
    818'.5402—dc21   99-048056

Printed in the United States of America

10 9 8 7 6 5

introduction

So it's come to this, then. You knew it would. Maybe from the moment you met her.

She is, of course, lovely. Yes. And many things besides, if we know you the way we think we do. She is smart and witty, curious and cunning. She is bold, brash, sweet, and shy. She is mysterious and vexing; brave and true. She'd rather wear cotton, but she wears satin as if she were born in it. And soon, so soon, she'll be enveloped in great, shimmering yards of the stuff, bunched and ruffled and blazing white, trailing somewhat ridiculously behind her and held out of puddles by an attending munchkin. It is astonishing, really, that you've found somebody you want to spend a lifetime with; more so by far that she wants the same. Outstanding. Congratulations.

But wait. Long before any such blissful celebration can be realized, before that short march that precedes the long, felicitous journey of a life well shared, there is much to do, and more to learn. Legions of friends and relatives must be assembled. Hundreds of choices made. Thousands of dollars procured and hemorrhaged. Do you, sir, have any idea how to select a ring? How much to pay for it? The rules governing tuxedos? The proper way to dissuade her from the tedious practice of using a hyphenated last name? Are you aware that a wedding is tantamount to the elevation of your bride to a deity for a day, while you remain decidedly a supporting actor? Are you steeled for the logistical precision essential to carrying off such a complex event, and grounded in the humility a groom must bring to the process? Are you ready for the years ahead, years of "reading the menu" but not "ordering," of compromise and discovery, of "meaningful" sex and panty hose on the shower rod?

Fear not—at least, not much. For in this succinct volume, we bring to bear the experience of thousands of men who have trod the marital road before you. We build on some traditions, tear down others, and present wedding lore that will gird you with the knowledge necessary to orchestrate the greatest day in your (and her) life. More important, perhaps, we offer advice on living as a couple, extending to the honeymoon and beyond. It is sound counsel, and we trust it will help you think of this institution as one that you, indeed, can't disparage. At least, not too often.

As the old Armenian toast goes, "May you grow old on one pillow."

—David Granger
Editor in Chief, *Esquire*

Esquire's
THINGS A
MAN
SHOULD KNOW ABOUT
MARRIAGE

Marriage upside:
No more boozy, rambunctious hunting for sex.

Marriage downside:
No more boozy, rambunctious hunting for sex.

East Indian Hindu couples are married before a small fire,
into which they toss flowers, water, seeds, and fruit,
which are considered the four symbols of life.

Here in the West, we have replaced this poetic custom
with a larger, metaphorical fire, into which we ritually
hurl great piles of currency.

An exercise in a most basic aspect of matrimonial preparedness:

Step One: In quiet moments, when alone, try substituting the phrase "my fiancée" for "my girlfriend."

Step Two: Attempt same in public.

Step Three: Make note of any involuntary gastric reactions to this utterance.

Step Four: Now try saying, "my wife." Repeat steps two and three.

The Wedding Timetable:
At least one year before the
date—find someone to marry.

Shortly thereafter, propose.

Around that time, if appropriate, start making little jokes about prenuptial agreements. (They're just jokes, honey!)

Note whether she laughs.

Disregard the above if she's the one with the trust fund.

Contrary to the Hollywood stereotype, prenuptial agreements are more often about protecting both your assets from the state and greedy divorce lawyers than about protecting a rich spouse from a poor one.

Sometimes prenuptial agreements are very much about protecting a rich spouse from a poor one.

Decent proposals: In private, on a starry night, preferably atop something tall—the Eiffel Tower, the Matterhorn, etc.

On bended knee: Optional.

Skip the bended-knee thing if there are lots of other people around—you don't need applause.

Besides, she might say no.

A preproposal suggestion: Glance inside her
hope chest. Scan for items of inordinate weirdness—
taxidermy, heroin works, ordnance, old boyfriends, etc.

You'll want to investigate her family as well,
since—trite but true—the nut doesn't fall far
from the tree.

Among adherents of the Friends Meeting,
a Quaker sect, couples wishing to be married
must first be investigated and approved by
the Clearness Committee.

You want to get to her hope chest before the
Clearness Committee does, we're thinking.

The Wedding Timetable: One year before the date—set the date. Also the budget. And the number of guests.

This would also be a good time to place an accredited psychotherapist on retainer.

High season for weddings: June and September.

Many things cost more during high season.

Consult the Farmers' Almanac before setting the date.

Recognize that almanacs are often wrong, and that outdoor weddings must always feature a tent.

The Wedding Timetable: One year before the date—
consider outsourcing wedding preparations to a
professional wedding consultant, armed with the
knowledge that, boy, will this person cost you.

If you have the money, pay for it.

Be sure you pick the right one.

Having done so, you may now discard
this book.

On second thought, donate it to one of your
groomsmen—he's bound to get his, someday.

The Wedding Timetable: Eleven months
before the date—having concluded that
you can't afford a wedding consultant,
get a huge, three-ring binder with dividers
and pockets and a calendar, and use this as
your central reference for all arrangements.

Be sure that your fiancée, not you, retains possession
of this book.

Indecent proposals: Anything involving blimps, skywriting,
fireworks, marching bands, contortionists, the Jumbotron at a
major-league sporting event, or submerging jewelry in crème
brûlée.

Jewelry shall not be hidden in any other sort of food
or drink. Including champagne.

Unless you don't mind capping off the perfect
romantic evening with the Heimlich maneuver.

Don't propose marriage when there's beer on your breath.

It is an excellent idea to sample the dozens of bridal magazines your fiancée will acquire.

Because besides clueing you in to the complex, fetishistic subculture of wedding planning, these magazines will have useful information about current fashions in tuxedos, flowers, photographers, etc.

Just don't read them in public.

The Wedding Timetable: Eleven months before the date—select a venue for the reception, check into the acoustics and the sound system before signing anything, and reserve your date.

Marriage: A community consisting of a master, a mistress, and two slaves—making in all, two.
—AMBROSE BIERCE

If you must know, Ambrose Bierce's marriage collapsed into an indefinite separation while he was employed to William Randolph Hearst, during which Bierce's wife perished.

Photographic symmetry aside, it does not matter whether you have the same number of bridesmaids as groomsmen.

Except that the wedding party generally proceeds into the church arm in arm.

And who's to say a couple of big guys in tuxes wouldn't make a darling couple?

The Wedding Timetable: One year before the date—select and reserve the photographer, florist, baker, caterer, and band or DJ for the reception.

You'll want to get references for photographers, florists, bakers, caterers, and bands or DJs for the reception.

Decide if the reception dinner will be a buffet or sit-down.

Buffet dinners cost just as much as sit-down dinners.

Sit-down dinners are better.

Because buffets generally involve chafing-dish fatigue, lack of food styling, and spending more time waiting in line for food than eating it.

In an ancient Roman wedding, the officiant sacrificed an animal, examined its entrails, and, based on this dissection, pronounced the gods' approval—or disapproval—of the union.

Marriage upside: Precious few denominations involve offal in their ceremonies these days.

The Wedding Timetable: One year before the date—reserve a block of hotel rooms for out-of-towners.

The Wedding Timetable: One year before the date—have an engagement portrait shot. Send it to the newspaper.

The Wedding Timetable: One year before the date—begin the long and arduous march toward the selection of a wedding dress.

For her.

You'll want to discuss the entire event carefully with your clergy of choice, so as to assure that he will: Conduct the wedding where you want to conduct the wedding, allow the music you want, allow the readings you want, allow people of varying religions to participate (like, say, your best man), and clarify any rules or restrictions, such as whether he requires one of you to convert to his denomination.

It is a classy—if outdated and sexist—custom to ask her father for her hand.

Presuming, of course, that she's not an amputee.

Careful: He may try to sell her to you, which is
not part of the tradition.

She doesn't have to know that you
sought his blessing.

And it will get you in good—really good—with her old man.

Available options, should her father refuse to give you
his blessing: (a) Wheedle in the general direction of her
mother to intercede; (b) Have him whacked; (c) Recognize
that it's none of his damn business.

Or you could elope.

Elopement upside: Most weddings are carefully engineered for the maximum embarrassment of the bride and groom at every opportunity.

Also: The father-in-law won't have expenses to grouse about, which you may one day be able to hold over his head.

Elopement downside: You become ineligible for the obscene cornucopia of booty that accompanies a formal wedding—that is, the gifts.

**The perfect elopement:
You, her, and a photographer
who will mail your parents
beautifully matted prints.**

Which your parents receive while you're honeymooning in Fiji.

The Wedding Timetable: Eight to ten months before the date—pick a honeymoon destination and check passports and inoculations, where appropriate.

The Wedding Timetable: Eight months before the date—register for gifts.

If you and your fiancée have lived together for a time and already have all the dish towels you need, feel free to register for gifts that are not housewares.

For example: Books, CDs, furniture, airline tickets, round lots of Microsoft stock.

Your wedding registry must include a good selection of inexpensive items.

Your wedding registry is something that your guests find out about by discreetly asking among themselves, not by reading it on the invitation.

Your wedding registry goes a long way toward thwarting the purchasing—and your subsequent returning—of Lava lamps, radial tires, and seventeen identical toasters.

The registry will not, however, be entirely successful in this regard.

Do not concern yourself overly about whether you like the presents you get— they are, after all, gifts, not an admission charge for your nuptials.

The groom's family pays for: Engagement ring, wedding bands, wedding license, preacher, rehearsal dinner, all flowers to be worn or carried by persons, honeymoon.

The bride's family pays for: Damn near everything else, including the invites, her dress, all flowers that are not worn or carried by people in the ceremony, the photographer, the reception.

If anything goes wrong with any of these, you must fix it.

Being too busy to fix anything on your own wedding day, you will in turn delegate such problems to the best man, who, it follows, must fix them.

The groomsmen and bridesmaids pay for (or rent) all their clothing for the wedding, and they do so at precisely the store you tell them to, when you tell them to.

All of the above payment traditions are out the window, obviously, if one or both families' finances so dictate.

The Wedding Timetable: Six months before the date—order wedding announcements, invitations, and thank-you notes.

Some couples have sent wedding invitations suggesting that guests pay a certain amount to attend. This is called extortion.

In 1999, a couple in the advertising business made headlines when they financed their wedding by selling ad space on their invitations, and on signs in the church and reception hall.

The bride, classy to the end, refused to sell ad space on the center aisle of the church—*that*, she said, would have been tacky.

Being your wedding, of course,
you get to invite whomever you want.

Believing the above statement to be true would reveal a degree of naïveté that, while touching, would call into question your preparedness for the institution of holy matrimony and the State Department level of diplomacy it requires.

Here is how it's gonna be:
Everybody she wants to receive
an invitation will receive an invitation.

Your fraternity brothers are not on that list.

Especially if they still answer to nicknames like
"Fridgeman" or "Hammerhead."

However, a small delegation of polite, gainfully employed
members of said brotherhood might escape her
attention (two, say).

The envelopes shall be addressed by hand.

It's nice to mention in the wedding program the name of the person who introduced the happy couple, especially if the introduction took place somewhere amusing.

The Betty Ford Clinic might not be amusing to everybody.

Marriage upside: You marry her money.

Marriage downside: You marry her MasterCard bill, student loans, and Saab payments.

Of course, you then have a nice little Saab at your disposal.

When reserving a block of hotel rooms for out-of-towners, make it clear to the hotel and the guests that this doesn't mean you're buying.

Because a lite beer from a minibar costs $7.50, that's why.

Here's how: On a card enclosed with the invitation and the directions, provide the name, address, and phone number of the hotel, and indicate the rate.

Conversely, if you're getting married on an island off the coast of Brazil where there are no hotels, the cost of the hut rentals fall to you.

Her family pays for the wedding reception.

You pay for the bride's bouquet, the moms' corsages, and those boutonnieres that make even the manliest of men look like Oscar Wilde.

And a gift for the bride. (Yes, another one.)

Nothing that plugs in.

If you're stuck, jewelry always works.

Give her the present before the wedding—after the rehearsal dinner, say.

Being the soon-to-be-spouse of a liberated woman,
you can fully expect her to share the cost of the
honeymoon with you.

However, she won't do so, because when it comes
to weddings, a woman's prerogative to revert to
presuffrage values is sacrosanct.

The Wedding Timetable: Six months
before the date—select and buy the rings.

Unless you're a Seventh-Day Adventist, in which case
your people aren't big on jewelry and generally eschew
wedding rings.

Design your own wedding rings?
Of course. If you're both wedding-ring
designers.

The DeBeers diamond cartel suggests in its
advertisements that men should spend two months'
salary on the engagement ring.

We don't know why; all we know is she sees those
advertisements.

Some women believe expensive diamond rings are
silly and excessive.

We've not yet met one.

That said, there are some alternatives to the traditional diamond ring.

Lifelong bachelorhood, among them.

Seriously, though: Ask your father and a couple of married male contemporaries of yours how much to spend.
Spend that much.

While it is thoughtful to let her pick out the ring, it is also gutless and infinitely less romantic than surprising her with one.

No matter what it is, she will like it.

If she doesn't like it, be grateful you're not marrying such a shallow, materialistic person.

Before purchasing said bauble, pilfer one of her existing rings—one she regularly wears on her ring finger—take it to a jeweler, and deduce her size.

The amount you spend on the ring indicates how much you can afford to spend on the ring, not how much you love its recipient.

The price for the same-quality diamond in the same-quality setting can vary as much as 300 percent, depending on where you buy it.

> Whether the stone even *is* a diamond can vary as much as 100 percent, depending on where you buy it.

A cubic zirconia, for example, looks exactly like a diamond to the untrained eye.

Don't even think about it.

The Wedding Timetable: Six months before the date—embark upon a short series of dance lessons.

Because you will be expected to dance
in front of everybody you know, and it's much
cooler to do so with style and aplomb than
to apologize for being a klutz.

Because those brides and grooms who are
able to execute a savage, floor-clearing tango
at the reception will create a breathtaking
moment that no one will ever, ever forget.

Especially if she spills out of her dress.

Or you split your pants.

Don't dip the mother-in-law unless you're
absolutely certain you won't drop her.

The Wedding Timetable: Six months before the date—choose
the formalwear for the ushers, groomsmen, and best man.

On the selection of the best man: For most grooms, it is imme-
diately obvious which of your friends deserves this honor.

What might be less obvious is the importance of this
individual's ability to handle the task.

The best man's primary duties: Deliver groom to all events at the correct time; supervise the groomsmen; put the kibosh on tasteless pranks; present an amusing toast at the reception; serve as manservant and therapist to the groom, who will occasionally fret about his decision to wed; and (oh, yes) keep track of the rings and the plane tickets for the honeymoon.

If such logistical adroitness is not your best friend's strong suit, pick your second-best friend and tell your best friend about all the labor you've spared him.

You must pretend convincingly to care about the china pattern over which your fiancée will agonize.

Because it validates her eventual choice of pattern, and because it attests to your sensitivity to her desire to have that choice validated.

> The Wedding Timetable: Four months before the date—complete the guest list. Procure guests' addresses. Place your orders with the (already reserved) caterer, orchestra, and florist.

> One guest-list philosophy: Decide who shall attend, and *then* figure out what you can afford to serve that many people.

When you make your first-draft guest list, rank each prospective guest as A-List, B-List, or C-List for purposes of elimination.

Avoid letting any of the guests see these lists—especially the C-listers.

Also, agree upon those D-list individuals who will receive mere wedding announcements.

Unless her father is loaded—and even then— you will have long and bitter fights about who will be on the guest list.

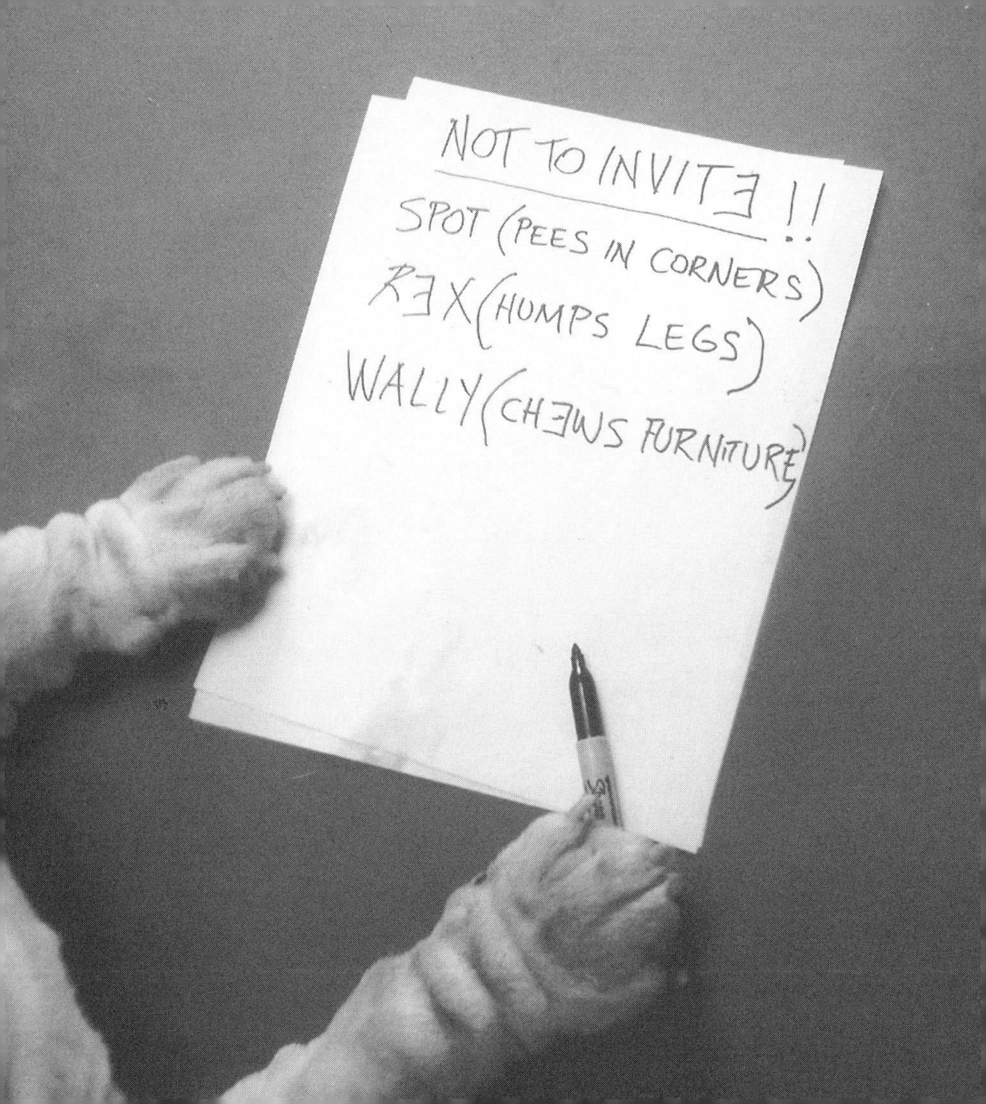
NOT TO INVITE!!
SPOT (PEES IN CORNERS)
REX (HUMPS LEGS)
WALLY (CHEWS FURNITURE)

Never start inviting people verbally before you
(er, she, actually) have penned the official guest list.

Invariably, you have already committed the
above faux pas—you must now invite those
people formally.

If you love your pal Bob but consider his girlfriend a shrew: You're screwed.

Because if you invite only Bob, he'll be offend-
ed that you snubbed his little friend.

You could, of course, blame the bride's family, or make it a practice across the board not to invite dates.

If Bob is married, you have no choice but to also invite his wife.

Children are not invited unless you itemize their names on the invitations.

Should people presume their children are invited anyway, what you do is tell them that no, in fact, they are not.

Your ex-girlfriends are not invited.

Her ex-boyfriends are generally not invited,
but are considerably more welcome than
your ex-girlfriends.

You don't have to invite stepparents if,
say, their marriage to your birth parent was
achieved through treacherous skullduggery,
or if they beat you with coat hangers—it's kind
of a case-by-case thing.

Sometimes, people will *ask* to be invited to your wedding.

This is unacceptable, and may be replied to along these lines: "We're having a really small wedding."

If that fails: "We're only allowed to have fifty people, and you wouldn't believe how many friends I can't invite—damn the bride's family!"

Avoid letting the bride hear you
blame everything on her family.

Better still, agree ahead of time that you're
both merely using mutual blame as an expedi-
ent way of telling peripheral acquaintances to
get lost.

In situations of looming, size-related budgetary
crises, one can also throw a less-formal party for
such peripheral friends in a bar one week
before the blessed event.

Make a list of things that you've hated from other people's weddings: The horse and carriage; the lack of liquor; excessive religious proselytizing; the lack of liquor; tuxedos that are not black; limos that are not black; bridesmaids' dresses that are lime green; the lack of liquor.

Don't allow those things.

Like it or not, you will defer to
your fiancée's wishes in all such matters,
and be a better man for it.

Think of it as premarriage practice for the rest of your life.

The Wedding Timetable: Three months before
the date—plan the music for the ceremony
and hire musicians.

The Wedding Timetable: Three months before
the date—plan the rehearsal dinner.

The rehearsal dinner is the first chance your
extended families have to break bread together, and thus should be arranged with care.

If you don't understand the gravity of this situation, imagine your aunt Geraldine regaling your new in-laws with tales of you wearing her stiletto heels.

Ask a close friend with a good eye to take a roll or two of candids during the rehearsal dinner, being sure to include everyone.

Develop these photos the next morning at a one-hour place and produce three small albums: One for her parents, one for your parents, and one for you and her to take on the honeymoon.

The Wedding Timetable: Three months before the date—
order the cake.

The Wedding Timetable:
Three months before the date—
arrange tuxedos and alterations.

A tuxedo, generally, is what the groom should wear.

A black one.

Because this isn't 1978.

Similarly, the limousine shall be of the ebony persuasion. Not white. Not even if the white one comes with a hot tub.

Especially if the white one comes with a hot tub.

The more fashionable formalwear shirt these days has a conventional collar, not a wing collar.

Pleats are optional. Ruffles are not.

It's cooler if the tuxedo for the groom is his own and not rented.

Cooler still if it was his father's.

Why you don't want to rent a tuxedo for the most important day of your life: Most formalwear rentals occur during prom season.

Do you remember what happened in *your* pants during prom season?

Should you opt for rented clothing, it is the best man's job to arrange for its pickup and return.

> Better: Require that groomsmen each purchase the same attractive, versatile suit of a color that a sane, but not stodgy, businessman would wear, such that it can be used again.

For example, a khaki-colored cotton number in summer, or charcoal gray in the cold months. Or blue blazers, say, and tan linen pants. And then, buy them matching neckties to wear for the ceremony.

Places to get married: A botanical garden,
Central Park, the seashore, City Hall,
a church, mosque, or synagogue.

Places to think twice about: Aloft in a hot-air balloon,
underwater in scuba gear, on top of Mount
Kilimanjaro, on the mound at Wrigley Field, or on a
speeding roller coaster.

Because if you get gimmicky,
her parents will hate you.

The Wedding Timetable: Two months
before the date—address invites.

Evening weddings are more formal than daytime weddings.

Indoor weddings are more formal
than outdoor weddings.

Winter weddings are more formal
than summer weddings.

While tradition holds that the most formal of weddings—
evening, in church—requires a tailcoat, this is just the sort of
tradition that was made to be violated.

If the groom cannot afford a tuxedo, or you desire a less-formal affair, a dark suit is an excellent and completely acceptable alternative.

The best man and ushers need not dress identically, as long as they're all in black tuxedos or all in dark suits.

Most men no longer wear tails because, aside from being uncomfortable, they make most men look like penguins.

You, sir, are most men.

If you like your boss,
invite him to your wedding.

If you fear your boss,
invite him to your wedding.

Don't worry about your boss ruining your wedding; you've got plenty of relatives and friends who are just as likely to do so.

On your wedding day, you'll speak to most guests for a maximum of three seconds—why worry?

The Wedding Timetable: Six weeks before the date—mail invites. Confirm florist. Negotiate seating chart.

About that seating chart: Employ sadistic pairings judiciously, as amusing as the idea may seem, because a brawl between your divorced parents isn't exactly the ambience you're after.

That said, it's okay to have a little fun. Alternating the seating of tall women with short men makes for good times on the dance floor.

The Wedding Timetable: Four weeks before the date—get the license. Call people who didn't RSVP. Confirm all vendors.

The Wedding Timetable: Four weeks before the date—buy gifts for groomsmen and bridesmaids, remembering that the best man and maid of honor get better gifts than the others.

A list of groomsman gifts recommended by an old guidebook that purports to help men prepare for weddings: Tie clips, handkerchiefs, address books, key rings, beach towels, small radios.

The above groomsman gifts suck.

Good groomsman gifts (which should be different for each guy, based on his interests; which is to say that, like all good gifts, they will require a measure of thoughtfulness about the recipient's interests): A Screwpull brand "Professional" model corkscrew, a wristwatch, small leather goods, single-malt whiskey, tickets to his favorite sports team, a silver Swiss Army knife from Tiffany.

The Wedding Timetable: Four weeks before the date—buy one of those guest books for people to sign.

Couples who are being married
for the second (or third, or fourth)
time often opt for a vastly simpler
and less expensive ceremony.

A toast for those enjoying their second
marriages: "A second marriage: To the
triumph of hope over experience."
—SAMUEL JOHNSON, 1770

The Wedding Timetable: Two weeks before
the date—send wedding announcement to
the newspaper. Reconfirm all honeymoon
reservations. Give your caterer the final
head count. Write your wedding program
and have it designed and printed.

Comic relief: Now and then, look back
at the original wedding budget and laugh
at your naïveté.

You can always call the whole thing off.

No, you don't get to keep the gifts.

The bachelor party, which you should be aware sometimes involves drinking noteworthy quantities of liquor, shall not occur any less than one solid week prior to the wedding day.

Recovery time, that's why.

Also re the bachelor party:
Drugs are avoidable.

Shots are avoidable.

Strippers are better in the abstract than when
they're directly, as it were, in your face.

Strippers are sometimes unavoidable.

Hookers are always avoidable.

Some bachelor parties have derailed
previously scheduled weddings because
the avoidable was not avoided.

You might want to choose your best man
based on the likelihood that he will take the
above fact into account.

Whatever it takes—be it hiring a limo, a fleet of taxis,
or a member of the recovery movement with a
Chevy Suburban—arrange so as no one imbibing at
the bachelor party ends up driving a motor vehicle.

You need not worry about what will happen
at the bachelorette party.

Because the bachelorette party is mostly
spent discussing what is happening at
the bachelor party.

Or so the bachelorettes always tell us—which is to say, maybe you should worry.

> Do not allow your future brother-in-law (or anyone else) to videotape the bachelor party, because everyone has his price, and your bride—not to mention *Hard Copy*—is ready to pay.

Create a diversion:
Send a male stripper-gram to the bridal shower.

That was a joke.

While we were just kidding, it actually might be pretty damned funny to send a stripper-gram to the bridal shower.

The Wedding Timetable: One week before the date—pick up rings. Write checks for the payment of your vendors and place them in envelopes for distribution at the reception.

The Wedding Timetable: One week before the date—get a haircut.

P.S. Spend more than $12 on it.

The Wedding Timetable: One day before the date—get a massage.

A legitimate massage.

Did we mention this? At some point in there, you should have found someone to wed.

As per prenuptial living together, there is that old adage, "Two rents before the ring."

Then again, rents were lower back then.

What to do when conservative in-laws expect you as-yet-unmarried lovebirds to sleep in separate rooms when visiting: Sleep in the same room.

Because allowing them that measure of control would set a hugely dangerous precedent.

Plus, it could get chilly.

That having been said,
sneaking into her room in the middle
of the night would be kind of hot.

What to use when the bed in the in-laws' guest room is squeaky: The floor.

You have opinions. Forget them.
Only hers count.

For example, if you're thinking about whether the incandescent hue of the boutonnieres matches the warm ochre tone of the cummerbunds, stop thinking about such things at once.

Couples considering marriage should rent the movie *Very Bad Things*, in which Cameron Diaz plays a spoiled psychotic fiancée who exhibits an unusual level of determination to have her wedding plans go her way.

Copious amounts of blood are spilled.

If this movie gives you ideas, you should see that therapist you put on retainer earlier.

> The Wedding Timetable:
> The day before the wedding—send flowers to wherever the bride is staying that night. Also, send flowers to your soon-to-be mother-in-law.

And don't let the groomsmen know where you're sleeping the night before the wedding, unless you relish the idea of receiving hourly pizza deliveries throughout the night.

THE BIG DAY

The Wedding Timetable: Ninety minutes before the ceremony—shower and dress.

Unless you're the bride, in which case, allow more like three hours—ditto for the bridesmaids.

Don't show up at the altar with wet hair.

Get up early enough to have time to dress, but not so early that you'll have too much downtime in which to panic.

That sudden flood of doubt in the morning when you wake—it's perfectly normal and will pass.

It hasn't? Repeat the following:
"There's always separation.
There's always divorce."

You probably don't want to say those things out loud.

And remember: She's afraid of commitment, too,
maybe just a little less so.

Remember also to confirm with your best man his continued
possession of the wedding rings.

Keep packages of Tums and Tylenol nearby during the ceremony—in one of the groomsmen's pockets, say.

If you've had a particularly checkered history, you might ask
the person performing your ceremony to omit the
"Speak now or forever hold your peace" bit.

There are those who advocate putting antiper-spirant on your hands to avoid sweaty palms.

Yes, that's what you want your hands to smell like on the most important day of your life.

No, it isn't.

Casting aspersions on the bride's entitlement to wear white during the ceremony is risky at best.

Unless, of course, the bride truly is a pregnant, beer-swilling slut.

Oh, for God's sake, of course that was a joke.

Mormon couples must become members of a temple and pay tithes for two years before church nuptials are allowed.

Only members-in-good-standing of the Mormon church are allowed to attend the wedding—a strict rule that includes even parents—but everyone's allowed at the reception.

Unitarian weddings: Anything, including all possible permutations of gender and sexual orientation, goes.

It is considered important in most human societies to arrive at the church in a timely fashion; we recommend it.

The Wedding Timetable: One hour before the ceremony—bridesmaids and groomsmen show up at the church for pictures, inspection of everyone's outfit, and the pinning of the boutonnieres.

To achieve this, they will have allowed enough driving time in the event of heavy traffic.

The Wedding Timetable: Thirty minutes before the ceremony—cue the organist to let fly with prelude music.

The Wedding Timetable: Thirty minutes before the ceremony—groom and best man arrive and hide in an out-of-the-way room, so as to smoke pot.

Quiz:
Which part of the preceding item is not true?

The groom's parents arrive approximately
fifteen minutes before start time.

The bride and her father also show up no less than
fifteen minutes out, and position themselves
in the preacher's office.

Bride's friends sit on the left of the aisle
(facing the altar). Groom's friends sit on
the right.

The ushers offer their right arm to seat guests.

Usually only when the guests are women.

If the groom's parents are divorced and remarried:
The groom's mother sits with the stepfather in the front pew.
The groom's father repairs to the third pew, with his wife,
if remarried. Same goes for sundered parents of the bride.

As you stand at the altar, before an assembly
of the most important people in your life, here
is what each and every one of them is staring
at and evaluating: Your haircut.

Don't sweat it. They're much more interested in her dress.

Still, it's all right to be nervous.

It's all right to wonder, however fleetingly,
whether you're making a terrible mistake.

It's not all right to soil your tuxedo.

Although if you do, it will be the one time
you'll be glad it was a rental.

And if it isn't a rental, you'll outgrow it
eventually anyway.

Make sure the officiant knows how
to pronounce your names.

At the altar: Have a handkerchief in your breast pocket,
at the ready.

In case she cries, knucklehead.

Or in case you cry, you big baby.

And because you don't want anybody grabbing the
officiant's vestments to blot spontaneous tears of joy.

Some clergy are so open-minded as to preside over a joint ceremony, such as one that involves bringing a Jewish "chuppah" into a Catholic church.

Some nuns probably bathe in a "mikvah," too—but not many.

A "chuppah" is a ceremonial canopy beneath which the happy couple stands with the rabbi.

"Mikvah" is the Hebrew word for string bikini.

No it isn't.

Military couples sometimes depart from the altar
through an arch of swords held aloft by fellow soldiers.

They do not, at such times, make references to Damocles.

Most clergy require couples to submit
to premarital counseling with them
before they'll perform a wedding.

Shockingly, most couples end up enjoying and
appreciating these sessions.

If you and your fiancée are of different religious
convictions, you'll want to discuss this potential source
of conflict *before* the wedding.

Particularly as pertains to your future children's religion.

Speaking of which, you'll want to discuss your thoughts about having children before you're wed.

You are more likely to faint during the ceremony than she is.

Fainting-avoidance strategies: Don't lock your knees, drink some water, make sure the air-conditioning works.

And eat something before the ceremony.

Not Italian sausage. Bananas, say.

The groom shall not grimace while pretending to screw the ring onto the bride's finger like a wing nut onto a carriage bolt.

Your wedding ceremony needn't be long. Particularly if we're invited.

The receiving line, if it must occur, happens on the way out of the church, where people are slightly less inclined to linger for ages.

Wedding pictures: Black and white is
more permanent and more romantic.

Spend more on the photographer than on the flowers.

Because photos last forever.

It's a wedding, not a basketball game:
Forget the videotaping.

Do you know anyone who has sat down to
review the videotape of his or her wedding?

You still need nice flowers.

What kinds of flowers to get:
This, friend groom, is not a decision
upon which you will be permitted input.

Spend more on the booze than the photographer.

There is no such thing as a cash bar
at a wedding.

Although there was a time in old England
when a bride's family was allowed to sell
ale at the ceremony to cover costs.

That time is past.

Should the beloved couple be unable to afford an
open bar, the best man should take it upon himself
to pass the hat or max out his credit cards or do whatever
it takes to make it happen.

Should he fail, no one shall be permitted to complain about it.

Anyone who can afford a wife can afford two kegs of Miller.

Anyone who has trouble affording two kegs of Miller should be having his reception in the backyard of whichever friend or relative has the nicest backyard.

Which actually sounds like a superb reception, especially if it was accompanied by a pig roast.

Graciously deflect prying questions from members of the bride's family about your plans to procreate.

Try, "We'll see! Ha-ha!"

Or, perhaps, "You first!"

All gifts will be accepted with ostensibly heartfelt gratitude—an act that should be carefully rehearsed for weeks.

Try this: "Excellent set of Victorian lace curtains, bro!"

It is not acceptable to request that gifts be accompanied by sales slips.

Fortunately, many stores will accept returns without receipts.

As for those that will not:
This is why we have attics and thrift stores.

No one dances with the bride before the groom
dances with the bride.

It is your reception. You decide what music will
be played. This needn't include "Celebration."

In part, because one hopes it's evident that
your wedding is, indeed, a celebration, and
that there is, indubitably, a party going on,
right here.

Nor should the featured numbers include
the Electric Slide or that chicken dance thing.

Make it clear to the band that you will
stop payment on the check, grant no tip,
and recommend them to no one if they
do not conform to your desire not to
hear such songs.

Also write into the contract that they're not
allowed to speak or ad-lib between songs.

Even if there's a fire.

Beware of the bandleader who wants to play "The Bride Cuts the Cake."

When the band plays the songs you specifically ordered them not to play—and they will—roll with it, hubby. You've got bigger fish to fry.

Irish Catholic weddings are as long as Irish Catholic receptions, but the receptions are so good, it's worth the wait.

Ditto for Italian weddings.

Baptist weddings are blissfully short, but then, the receptions are often dry.

It follows that the best wedding events involve a Baptist girl marrying an Irish boy.

Jewish receptions are also excellent, especially that part when the overenthusiastic guests hoist the bride and groom (and sometimes parents) in chairs above their heads and totter them about the dance floor to the strains of "Hava Nagila," a scenario of exhilarating danger.

To the vegetarians in our midst:
This is your one and only chance to
exact revenge upon your meat-eating friends:
They will eat hummus and babagannouj
at the reception, and they will like it.

You don't let just any old friend toast you at the reception.

You know those astonishingly humiliating toasts you've seen
drunk guys give at other people's weddings? That's why.

The order of the garter is a tradition born of the days of King Arthur, when a lady bestowed a ribbon upon the knight who carried her colors into battle.

The garter is worn just below the bride's knee.

Below the knee, we said.

The groom then tosses the garter. Someone catches it.

If he sniffs it, deck him.

Make a toast to your bride.

You can make it funny, but beware—if it's too flip or sarcastic, you'll pay for it later.

No one ever got in trouble for making a sweet toast.

Like this one: "Grow old with me! The best is yet to be,
The last of life, For which, the first is made."
                                        —ROBERT BROWNING

Armenian wedding toast: "May you grow old on one pillow."

It has been scientifically proven that wearing a bridesmaid's dress generates a frothy combination of lust and bride-envy from which dapper groomsmen are the most likely to profit.

No groomsmen shall sleep with the bride's little sister.

Of course it's not your fault,
but you're the one who'll get blamed.

**The wedding kiss:
Of some duration and sincerity,
laden as it is with meaning.**

But not a full-on tonsil-tickling snog.

Drinking guideline for the groom:
One drink for every two glasses of water.

Drinking guideline for the bride:
As much as she wants, since as tough
as this day might be for you, it's even
more so for her.

Correction, there, seeing as how a sloppy bride
is not pretty: Assign one cousin to keep her
champagne glass full all night, and another
cousin to stop the first one if your bride is start-
ing to drool onto her dress.

Also, make sure the bride eats.

Since you'll be spending most of the night dancing
and partying, your opportunity to eat may pass you by.

Which is why it's not a bad idea to stay in a hotel
that has room service.

Plus, you get to have breakfast in bed the next morning.

The bride will likely hold a bridesmaids' lunch
on the day of the wedding.

You should plan an activity for you and your groomsmen during this time.

Okay as activities: Golf, Frisbee, a swim in a nearby lake.

Not-okay activities: Skydiving, tequila shots, one last trip to the strip club.

Places to honeymoon: Napa. Tuscany. Loire Valley.

Places not to honeymoon: Branson. Toledo. Any country under martial law. Any city with a Six Flags.

Allow at least an hour for the tying of
your bow tie, and have someone with
nimble fingers available to help.

That goes double for the groomsmen.

At the ceremony: Two or three readings of the literary or bibli-
cal persuasion are nice.

Think twice about allowing relatives to sing, play acoustic
guitar, recite original poetry, or, particularly, to sing, play
acoustic guitar, AND recite original poetry.

Under no circumstances permit the performance of the song "I Gave My Love a Cherry"—not even if you wrote it.

No flutes. No tubas.

Think twice about writing long, earnest, gooey vows.

Because, apart from nauseating your guests, excessive sentiment is more likely to make you sob embarrassingly at the altar.

The "suggested donation" requested by
your clergyman is not merely "suggested."

Further, the amount of the "suggested donation"
is best exceeded slightly.

You want him to put in a good word for you with The Man, no?

Tell no one where you're spending your wedding night.

Except the bride.

Before the wedding, hide your car.

Because it's a hassle to scrape soap off your windows and untie strings of cans from your bumper.

Before the wedding, hide your girlfriend.

That was a joke.

Disposable cameras: On the tables.
At the reception. Not the ceremony.

And especially not in lieu of a professional photographer.

Because there is no substitute for a good—a really, really good—professional photographer.

List the photos you want taken—college friends, specific family shots, etc., or you'll find that you got no shots of Uncle Vito with Aunt Marge.

Also, encourage the photographer
to take plenty of candids.

Set a time limit for the photographer to take the posed pictures. (A half hour is a good benchmark, unless you have a
really big family.)

Friends who offer to sing a cappella at your
wedding/videotape your wedding/cater your
wedding—do you want to remain friends with
these people? Thank them and decline.

The groom's cake: A nice tradition that will result in
a tuxedo pocket full of butter-cream frosting.

Rice or birdseed: Throw birdseed, not so much because rice will choke birds, but because people *think* rice will choke birds.

If you're considering releasing live butterflies instead of throwing birdseed, reconsider.

Because invariably a third of the insects will turn out to be dead in their little boxes, the discovery of which will cause a faint but unmistakable gloominess among the unlucky guests that receive them.

Have a chilled bottle of champagne waiting for you in the honeymoon suite.

Relax and enjoy it—it will all be over so, so soon.

'TIL DEATH DO YOU PART

Some folks insist that, for them, the honeymoon never ends.

These people were supposed to stop taking Halcion as soon as the reception was over, but evidently had refills.

On the honeymoon:
Relax, enjoy everything, roll with problems,
don't sweat small things, and don't argue.

Everybody argues on their honeymoon.

Don't argue on hotel balconies.

It's not necessarily a bad sign if the bride
cries during the honeymoon.

Or the groom.

Make no comments about the number of shoes she brings.

Arrange for your connubial dwelling
to be available as soon as you return
from your honeymoon.

Marriage upside:
On those chilly nights, a surefire heat source.

Marriage downside:
Fighting for the covers.

Mandatory minimum: Queen-size bed.

Highly preferable: King-size bed.

Thank-you notes are handwritten,
gift-specific, and mailed within a week
of your return from the honeymoon.

Wedding presents theoretically can arrive within a year
of your nuptials.

Wedding gifts that arrive eleven months after your wedding
date require a commensurately less-punctual thank-you note,
we're thinking.

Don't feel bad about returning wedding gifts.
Exult—it's part of the deal.

On the honeymoon:
Perform sexual acts as much
as you wish.

But remember—no one's keeping score.

As she is now your wife, you will not tell
your buddies of anything that might qualify
for the record books.

Draw comfort from the fact that a notable percentage of couples tumble into bed so exhausted on their honeymoon night
that they can manage nothing more acrobatic than a kiss.

You'll of course be expected to lie about this in the future.

The man said for better or for worse.

And it can get bad. Real bad.

Like when your father-in-law passes on and your wife's mother, alone for the first time in thirty-five years, proposes moving in with you.

It is better for the two of you to pick out a new home together than for one of you to move into the other's home.

Because the newcomer will invariably feel like a guest in the other person's castle.

Marriage downside: Her cats.

Marriage upside: Cats are excellent playthings for your dog.

If she insists on hyphenating your last names:
Suggest that she keep hers.

If she still insists on hyphenating your names:
Suggest that you take hers.

Under no circumstances agree to an arrangement in which anyone is utilizing hyphenated names.

Because they're manifestly irritating to the thousands of people who, for the rest of your lives, will have to write them down—that's why.

Some people—for instance, Jenny Kruzmanic and Will Winegarten of Sioux Falls—have proposed eliminating this problem by combining their names into Kruzgarten or Winemanic.

Will and Jenny have a terrible marijuana problem.

Married people need life insurance.

Life insurance is *not* an investment; it provides cash to your family in the event of your untimely death, so that they can continue to eat and make house payments.

> How much insurance you need:
> Just enough to provide for the family in
> your absence, but not so much that you are
> more valuable to them dead than alive.

That was a joke.

But watch your back.

For specifics: Get a broker.

Married people need wills, and they
need them right now.

Married people with lots of money are often
better off with a revocable living trust than
with a will.

Do-it-yourself will kits could save you hundreds
of dollars when you write your will, and could
cost your heirs thousands of dollars in
unnecessary taxes.

Which is to say: Get a lawyer.

Remember how before the wedding, you did things with your friends and she did things with her friends? This should continue, albeit less often.

Many women do not like ice fishing, golf, bowling, or poker, which is why every man must take up at least one of these hobbies, because, while uninteresting, they allow for the women-free consumption of liquor and the unfettered discussion of, you know, women.

There must be a regular boys' night out.

More important—and much more often—there must be couples' nights in.

Schedule a special time in which you light candles, put on some Yanni, hold hands naked, stare deeply into each other's eyes, and discuss how to come up with eight grand for the new cabinets.

There is no such thing as a sophisticated, cultivated man who cannot cook something.

Unless he is impossibly rich.

So learn.

Then, cook something for her now and then.

When someone else has cooked for you, no matter how wretched the food actually was, it was delicious.

And you wash the dishes.

There are few relationship troubles that cannot be solved with Häagen-Dazs.

While the above statement may sound astonishingly condescending, it remains true.

Those troubles that cannot be solved with Häagen-Dazs—well, as Keanu Reeves might say, "Whoa."

A husband needs a den.

A wife needs her husband to have a den, if only to have a place to banish his bachelor furniture.

Marriage downside: Even if you have a den, she will seek to discard your stuff.

Marriage upside: She's right about the painting of the dogs playing pool.

Also the KISS posters.

She's wrong about the recliner.

And the more she wants to throw it out,
the wronger she becomes.

She also will attempt to discard some of
your favorite clothes.

She will be correct about some of them,
but not all, which is why you must
fight for each one.

She's wrong about the cap from your college baseball team.
She's right about the Jägermeister T-shirt.

Don't want to wear a wedding band? Sorry, pal—you don't
have a choice.

Of course, you could remind her of how most single women
find a little gold ring on a man's left hand the world's most
powerful aphrodisiac.

Women think they're neater than men.
Not all of them are.

Many women wish to redecorate their first
marital home, which is a project the two of you
should share, although it is advisable to eventually
acquiesce on most points of contention.

Unless she wants wallpaper borders with
little ducks on them.

Or she wants you to sleep in a canopy bed.

It is unacceptable for you (or her) to throw away items that you (or she) might find offensive but that she (or you) may love.

Marriage downside: In-laws, primarily the unavoidable squandering of valuable vacation time on visits to them.

Marriage upside: In-laws.
(You might like them.)

In the event that you don't like them, they may still come in handy as baby-sitters, and there's something good about that.

Oh, yes: Children, a frequent by-product of marriage.

Before the children arrive: Get in a little traveling, career-building, sleeping, sex—that sort of thing.

Should you not like the in-laws, remember that she has in-laws, too, and it's fifty-fifty that she feels the same way you do about hers.

How to approach in-laws: You're an anthropologist. They're anthropoids. In their own special way, they are fascinating. Study.

Should you deduce that the in-laws are repellent: (a) Learn to fake it, and (b) Present alternate vacation options so irresistible that your wife, too, will desire to blow her parents off.

When this doesn't work, it is best to spend the better part of the first year saying little and listening much.

Things to discuss with her family: Their excellent interpretations of regional cuisine, their favorite sports teams, their beautiful house, their new car, their lawn.

Things not to discuss with her family: Abortion, your criminal record, legalization of drugs, gays in the military, polygamy, your kinky fascination with the movie *Crash*.

On the subject of conflict: Sometimes you must agree to disagree.

For instance, she may never understand why you can't just always use the toilet in a seated position.

Look, the simple fact is, you'll never win the hackneyed seat up/seat down argument, and wouldn't you rather avoid it altogether?

Speaking of fights, it's better to piss her off
than to piss off her best friend or her mother.

Because her best friend can instantly and
irrevocably undermine her devotion to you.

Because her mother will poison your children
against you.

Because the Häagen-Dazs clause will work
on your wife, but not on her mom or her
confidante.

Before we forget:
Your Little Black Book goes into the shredder.

You can read the menu, but you can't order.

You had better not read the menu too often or too carefully.

Most couples these days have a policy of
permitting sex outside the marriage,
so long as the other partner
doesn't know about it.

You wish.

"There is nothing nobler or more admirable
than when two people who see eye to eye
keep house as man and wife, confounding
their enemies and delighting their friends."
—HOMER, *THE ODYSSEY*

Having gotten married, you might want to
divest yourself of some of those extensive
pornography holdings.

Or keep them in the den.

Locked.

Women love to wear your shirts. Let them.

Women love to wear your sweaters, which can stretch them out in the breast region. Let them.

And be thankful you're married to a woman who has a figure that stretches out your sweaters in the breast region.

**Cheating on your wife
is never worth it.**

Cheating on your wife is actually worse
for you if she has no idea you did it.

In some ways.

Not others.

If you cheated on your wife:
(a) Don't tell her,
(b) Don't tell anybody else, and
(c) Never do it again.

Because: As you unburden yourself of your guilt, you burden her with a horrible sense of betrayal, and eventually, anyone you tell will tell somebody else.

For Pete's sake, why did you get married if you're still compelled to play the field? Give her an enormous settlement, toss this book, and go back to the tomcattin' you love.

Women believe that the production of children is the best way to cause you to finally grow up and behave yourself. And, as usual, they are correct.

Because most kids are an indescribable joy—even better than Monday night football—and women know you'll figure this out as soon as you've got the little bug in your ever lovin' arms.

Marriage upside: Dual incomes.

Marriage downside:
The inevitability of fighting about money.

Early on, the in-laws, too, need to learn a few rules, chief among them: No unannounced visits.

One way to inculcate folks with the appropriate values as per visits is to repeat the following: "Well, we'll always call before we come over—we'd hate to interrupt your frequent lovemaking."

The lovemaking part was a joke.

Another way: Refuse to give them a key.

In-laws also need to be schooled as to their role in the decoration of your house, the rearing of your kids, and the direction of your career, which is: A very small and strictly advisory one.

Know that for a while it will be an interesting
and amusing experience to use the phrase,
"my wife."

Call her "The Old Ball-and-Chain" in front of your friends— she'll like that.

A phone number that might come in handy
in the aftermath of calling her that:
1-800-D-I-V-O-R-C-E.

Meantime, keep smiling.

We know it sometimes hurts,
but you've got no choice:
Keep smiling.